Litecoin

An Introduction to Litecoin Cryptocurrency and Litecoin Mining

Jeff Reed

Copyright 2017 – Jeff Reed. All rights reserved.
The information in this book represents only the view of the author. As of the date of publication, this book is presented strictly for informational purposes only. Every attempt to verifying the information in this book has been done and the author assumes no responsibility for errors, omissions, or inaccuracies.

In no way is it legal to reproduce, duplicate, or transmit any part of this document in either electronic means or in printed format. Recording of this publication is strictly prohibited and any storage of this document is not allowed unless with written permission from the publisher. All rights reserved.

Respective authors own all copyrights not held by the publisher.

The information herein is offered for informational purposes solely, and is universal as so. The presentation of the information is without contract or any type of guarantee assurance.

The trademarks that are used are without any consent, and the publication of the trademark is without permission or backing by the trademark owner. All trademarks and brands within this book are for clarifying purposes only and are the owned by the owners themselves, not affiliated with this document.

Contents

Introduction 1

Chapter 1 Litecoin 101 3

Chapter 2 Benefits And Risks Involved 22

Chapter 3 Risks Involved 31

Chapter 4 Getting Started 39

Chapter 5 Litecoin Wallet 45

Chapter 6 Buying Litecoin 54

Chapter 7 Litecoin Mining 65

Chapter 8 Tips For Investing 88

Other Books From The Author 95

Introduction

We live in the age of digital currency. CryptoCurrency is no longer an obscure concept. In the month of June 2017, a single Bitcoin was valued at more than $2000. The world of CryptoCurrency isn't just restricted to Bitcoins! Did you know that there are about 180 currencies that are in circulation and are recognized internationally? Just like ordinary currency, different types of cryptocurrencies are in existence too. Since Bitcoin happens to have been the first CryptoCurrency, it enjoys more publicity than the rest. However, the buck doesn't stop there. Litecoin is the new form of digital currency on the block, and it is poised for dynamic growth.

Initially, the world of cryptocurrencies might seem intimidating. If you are equipped with the right information, you can make an informed decision. There are plenty of cryptocurrencies to choose from. However, investing in Litecoin is a smart move. In this book, you will learn more about what Litecoin is all about, the way it came into existence and some of its basic features.

So, what are we waiting for, let's get started!

Chapter 1

Litecoin 101

In October 2013, Charles Lee, a former Google engineer, unveiled Litecoin. Litecoin was introduced as the "silver" to the "gold" of Bitcoin. Lee had come up with the idea of Litecoin to fix the problems that Bitcoins posed. Litecoin is amongst the top 5 digital currencies that are present in the market and is considered to be a fierce rival of Bitcoin. Litecoin, like several of its counterparts, functions as an online payment system like PayPal or any banking application. Users can easily conduct transactions using CryptoCurrency. Only instead of using fiat currency like the U.S. dollar, the transaction is carried out in units of Litecoin.

Initially, the world of cryptocurrencies might seem intimidating. If you are armed with the correct information, you can make an informed decision. There are plenty of cryptocurrencies to choose from. However, thinking about investing in Litecoin is a smart move. In this chapter, you will learn more about what Litecoin is all about, the way it came into existence and some of its basic features.

Here are a few facts about Litecoin. There are four times as many Litecoins as Bitcoins. This means that there are 84 million Litecoins in circulation. A greater number of Litecoins signifies smaller blocks that need to be mined. Smaller blocks will need fewer confirmations. Thereby making Litecoin transactions faster than Bitcoin transactions. Litecoins are more secure when compared to their counterparts. There are plenty of Litecoins in circulation. Even if you missed your chance with Bitcoins, it isn't late to jump onto the Litecoin bandwagon.

How is Litecoin made?

A government does not issue Litecoin, like the other cryptocurrencies. The government has singularly been the entity throughout the history that has been responsible for minting money. The Federal Reserve doesn't regulate Litecoins, and they aren't minted at a press at the Bureau of Engraving and Printing. Litecoins are created by a complicated process referred to as mining. This process comprises the processing and verification of several Litecoin transactions. Unlike fiat currency, there is a cap on the number of Litecoins present. There can be no more than 84 million Litecoins in circulation. A block is generated on the Litecoin network in every 2.5 minutes. The block is made up of ledger entries of Litecoin transactions that take place around the world. This is where a Litecoin derives its value. The block of transactions is verified by using mining software and is visible to any miner who wishes to see it. Once a block is verified, the next block will enter the chain, and this will contain the record of all the Litecoin transactions ever transacted. Whenever a block is mined, certain number of Litecoins is handed over to the miner as a reward.

Mining for Litecoin

The incentive offered for mining is that for every block that is successfully verified, 25 Litecoins are awarded. Initially, the number of Litecoins offered as a reward were 50 and from October 2015, it's been reduced to 25. This process of reduction will keep on recurring until all the 84 million Litecoins are mined. Will an unscrupulous miner change the algorithm of the block and enable double spending? Well, this isn't possible and any attempt made to do so can be spotted immediately by the other miners. The identity of any miner that detects such an irregularity is always anonymous.

The only way the entire blockchain network can be disrupted in will be if a majority of miners agree to process the false transactions, this is practically impossible to achieve. Mining CryptoCurrency at a rate that can be considered to be profitable to the miner will need a lot of processing power and specialized hardware. Your regular laptop isn't designed to be fast enough to complete this task.

This is where Litecoins differ from their competitors. Any off-the-shelf computers can mine Litecoins. However, a machine with a greater processing power can help in increasing the chances of earning some Litecoins.

Mining is a task that can be done individually or collectively. Whenever a group of miners get together for the purposes of mining, it is referred to as pooling. It is easier to mine when there is better and more powerful technology at a miner's disposal. Whenever a miner from such a pool mines a block, the reward will also be distributed amongst the other miners in a proportion that's been agreed beforehand.

Value of Litecoin

Any currency and even the gold bullion are only as valuable as the society perceives it is. If the Federal Reserve increases the circulation of all the dollars in the market, then the value of the dollar is bound to plummet. This phenomenon isn't just restricted to currency. When the supply of any good or service increases, then there will be a reduction in its value. The creators of Litecoin were aware of this. They knew it would be difficult for a new currency to build a good reputation for itself. However, by restricting the number of Litecoins in supply, the founders managed to put people's fear about overproduction to rest. A currency is devalued whenever its production increases. This rule of economics doesn't govern Litecoin. Since there is a cap on the number of Litecoin that can exist in the market. However, their value will solely depend on the users and how valuable the society thinks they are.

In a way, Litecoins are derived from Bitcoins. You can obtain Litecoins by creating an account for trading your Bitcoins for Litecoins at an online exchange for cryptocurrencies. You must be wondering why you should trade one CryptoCurrency for another? There are certain advantages that Litecoin has got over Bitcoins. Litecoin is capable of handling a greater number of transactions because the time required for the generation of a block is less. The transaction fee is less as well. So, the value of Litecoin is dependent on the perception of the society. The most reliable store of value during a crisis will be the currencies used. During the late 1990s and early 2000s, Zimbabwe was stricken by hyperinflation, and the Zimbabwean dollar had become worthless. Everyone who was holding any form of liquid assets suffered a significant loss. This scenario is almost impossible to think about when using Litecoins because of the cap on the number of Litecoins in circulation.

Once a currency has reached is being utilized by a significant chunk of the population and people are confident about what it represents, then in such a case, it will be able to sustain itself. However, Litecoin has got a long way to go before it can support itself as a method of payment. Cryptocurrencies are rapidly gaining popularity, and Litecoin has got immense potential.

Why is Litecoin unique?

Bitcoin has a leg up on its competition since it was the first digital currency created. However, its early arrival has also resulted in a couple of drawbacks. Developers of all the major cryptocurrencies have managed to identify the weaknesses present in Bitcoins and tweak their currencies for overcoming these shortcomings. Bitcoin was the first one to use Blockchain technology. However, Litecoin has managed to overcome certain issues that plagued its predecessor.

The foundation of all cryptocurrencies in existence is the Blockchain technology. Every transaction that takes place in the network of digital currencies is recorded within a block. All these blocks are linked together to form a literal chain. Anyone on the network has access to the information that is present on this Blockchains. This implies that the transactions are available for public viewing, even if the user is anonymous. This framework helps in making cryptocurrencies secure. Litecoin uses this technology more efficiently. On the Litecoin network, a new block is generated every 2.5 minutes, which is 7.5 times faster than the Bitcoin network. All those merchants who are looking for faster transactions will find this appealing. Transactions with Litecoin aren't just swift; they are secure as well. Segregated Witness, popularly known as SegWit was activated in the blockchain network of Litecoin. In this process, obtaining signature data from transactions breaks down the blocks in a blockchain. Litecoin can process lightning-fast payments because of this. In the world of CryptoCurrency, only a finite number of coins can exist. There cannot be more than a specific number of Bitcoins that are present in the world. The same rule applies to Litecoins as well. However, the number of coins present can vary, and this works in Litecoin's favor.

The Scrypt algorithm that Litecoin makes use of makes it easier for miners to access the network. This can have two outcomes. The first one is that it will encourage more miners to participate in the Litecoin network. This will help in promoting the usage of Litecoin since it is attractive to all those users who never got an opportunity to mine Bitcoin. The simplicity of the Litecoin mining process is attractive to Bitcoin miners. Bitcoin mining needs specialized supercomputers, and these algorithms are just increasing in complexity. So, all those miners who are tired of struggling with Bitcoin mining can shift to Litecoin now.

How to invest?

Litecoin is a powerful digital currency, and with the way that it is progressing, it has a lot of potential. If you are thinking about investing in Litecoin, then now is the time. You can purchase these from any of the exchanges or mine them. More information about both these methods has been provided in the coming chapters. So, read on to find more!

As mentioned earlier, Litecoin was developed as an alternative to Bitcoin to address some of its shortcomings. Litecoin is lightweight and is more abundant in the market when compared to Bitcoin. The proof-of-work algorithm used by Litecoin is Scrypt, and this algorithm is almost immune to ASIC mining. You will learn more things about getting started with Litecoins in the coming chapters. Here are a few things that you should take into consideration before buying Litecoin.

- This CryptoCurrency has become quite popular amongst the speculators in the market after the price surge that the Bitcoin experienced in November 2013. The prices of these cryptocurrencies might move similarly. However, the prices of Litecoin are comparatively lower.
- The infrastructure of Litecoin is relatively less developed than that of Bitcoin. This might not be a problem for a seasoned investor, but a novice investor might take a while to figure things out.

- You can earn Litecoins by mining them by using standard computing equipment.
- Always do plenty of research on your own, before investing your hard-earned money, and never take on more risk than that you can shoulder. Don't be emotional while making an investment decision; only make it when you know you won't be at the losing end.

Cash for Litecoins or Bitcoins for Litecoins

Once you have made up your mind about buying Litecoins, you will need to decide whether you will want to buy these in exchange for fiat currency or Bitcoins. The infrastructure of Litecoin isn't as developed as that of Bitcoin. The easiest manner in which you can acquire Litecoins will be by buying them with Bitcoins. This is the fastest method, and for most of the users, this is cost effective as well. If you are holding Bitcoins, then you can make use of these for buying Litecoins from any of the listed exchanges like BTC-e, Kraken, Cryptsy, and other exchanges. The process of buying Litecoins is yet to be streamlined. There are about two dozen exchanges that deal in Litecoins and most of them allow for only Bitcoin to Litecoin transactions or vice versa. A couple of exchanges like Bitfinex, Crypto-Trade, Kraken, and BTC-e sell Litecoins for fiat currency (dollars, euros, and rubles only). However, the availability will depend on your location. For instance, in the UK, investors have the option of directly buying Litecoins from Bittylicious or BitBargain via a banking transfer. However, this isn't the case in most countries.

It might seem straightforward to purchase Litecoin by a fiat wire transfer, but this can be quite tedious. Some of the major Bitcoin exchanges aren't yet open to the idea of trading in Litecoin. The obvious advantage of buying Litecoin with Bitcoin should be speed. Theoretically, this just takes a couple of minutes; whereas international wire transfers can take up to a few days and these transfers are usually subjected to several additional costs as well. There aren't many Litecoin exchanges, and this means that all the interested investors will have to rely on international transfers. A viable alternative would be buying Bitcoin locally, thereby skipping the hassle of international money transfer, and converting the same into Litecoin.

Differences between Litecoin and Bitcoin

In the year 2009, Satoshi Nakamoto came up with world's first CryptoCurrency, Bitcoin. The code used is an open source. This means that it could be modified by anyone and could be freely used for different projects. Different cryptocurrencies have been launched ever since, and each of these makes use of a modified version of this code. Litecoin was initiated in the year 2011, and it was referred to as being "silver" to Bitcoin's "gold." If you take a cursory glance at both these currencies, they seem quite similar.

Just like Bitcoin, Litecoin was intended to facilitate peer-to-peer transactions. The holders of Litecoins can make payments and perform any transactions anywhere in this world without worrying about any additional fees. Litecoin operates as globally accepted currency and thereby gets rid of the need to adjust its value while exchanging money anywhere in the world. Litecoin is decentralized. No central authority is responsible for it, and the currency can flow freely on the World Wide Web. It certainly is more secure than fiat currency. There is no governmental interference regarding its production and regulation.

The value of Litecoin rests in the hands of its users. Like any other form of digital currency that is available, even Litecoin needs to be "mined." Miners make use of computers for processing Litecoin transaction that is represented by algorithms solvable by computers. Whenever an algorithm is solved, additional Litecoins are introduced into the network, and the miner will be rewarded with 25 Litecoins. There is a finite number of Litecoins in existence, and the total volume of Litecoins cannot exceed 84 million.

Once that point is reached, the coin can be broken down into smaller payments. The mining processes, along with the cap on the number of Litecoins present, help in protecting this currency from hyperinflation. Litecoin is capable of regulating itself. Every time a transaction is verified on the network, the network becomes more secure. So, it does seem like Bitcoin and Litecoin are similar in a few ways, but then they are quite different too. In this section, let us look at the differences that exist between Litecoin and Bitcoin.

The most basic difference between these two will be the coin limit. There are 21 million Bitcoins whereas there are 84 million Litecoins present. Bitcoins run on SHA-256 algorithm whereas Litecoin runs on Scrypt. There are mining differences between Litecoin and Bitcoin. Mining just like Bitcoins generates Litecoins. In the year 2011, Charles Lee, a former Google engineer, developed Litecoin. The main idea of the Litecoin is to work on overcoming the drawbacks of Bitcoin. A significant difference between these two for the end user is the time to generate a block of Litecoin is 2.5 minutes while the Bitcoin takes 10 minutes.

From the perspective of miners and enthusiasts, there is another point of difference between Litecoin and Bitcoin, and this is the proof of work algorithm that these two cryptocurrencies make use of. Like mentioned earlier, Bitcoin makes use of a SHA-256 hashing algorithm that involves calculations, which can be accelerated in parallel processing. This feature is the reason for the rise of increased competition in ASIC technology and has also lead to an increase in the difficulty level of Bitcoin mining. Litecoin makes use of Scrypt algorithm; formerly known as S-crypt and pronounced as "script." This algorithm has managed to incorporate SHA-256 that Bitcoin runs on and its calculations are more serialized than compared to its predecessor.

Instead of just raw processing power, large amounts of RAM with high-speed are favored by Scrypt. This is the reason why Scrypt is referred to as memory hard problem. There hasn't been much competition in mining for Litecoin because of this algorithm and also because there isn't ASIC technology that is available. There is a huge difference between the hashing power of these two cryptocurrencies. The hashing rate of the Bitcoin network is 20,000 terra hashes per second when compared to 95,642 mega hashes per second on the Litecoin network. The mining rigs for Litecoin are available in the form of customized PCs that have multiple graphic cards fitted into them. These devices are capable of handling calculations that are required for running the Scrypt algorithm and has access to high-speed memory that is incorporated into their circuit boards.

There are transaction differences between these two cryptocurrencies as well. Litecoin is capable of confirming transactions quicker than Bitcoin, and this has several implications. Litecoin is capable of handling transactions of a higher volume because of its quicker block generation. If Bitcoin were to match up to this, then the Bitcoin's code will need some serious updates. The volume of blocks on the Litecoin blockchain network is more than that present on the Bitcoin blockchain. There is a reduction in the risk of double spending with Litecoin because of the faster block time. A merchant will have to wait for five minutes to receive two confirmations whereas the wait time will have been ten minutes for just one confirmation with Bitcoins.

Chapter 2

Benefits and Risks Involved

Why are Litecoins popular? Here are the different benefits that Litecoins have to offer.

Financial self-determinism

The Litecoin network is a unique ecosystem, and it helps in digitally storing value. Users can save their valuable Litecoins in wallets that are secure. They can transact without having to rely on middlemen or other regulatory authorities. It is almost impossible for hackers or banks to take your Litecoins away from you, once you acquire and secure them. The government cannot freeze your Litecoin account, and it certainly cannot prevent you from transacting on the Litecoin network. Whenever you purchase with your credit card, then you will be giving the vendor or the merchant access to your credit line, regardless of the quantum of the transaction. Credit cards usually operate on this basis. This means that once the store has initiated the payment, then the assigned amount will be automatically pulled from your concerned account. CryptoCurrency, on the other hand, makes use of a push technique. This means the holder of CryptoCurrency will need to authorize the transaction before it can be processed.

Transactions are irreversible

A transaction that has been conducted using CryptoCurrency like Litecoin is irreversible. A major problem that most of the retail vendors face is chargebacks. Most of the usual payment options like credit cards, interbank transfers, or even PayPal have provisions that will allow a customer to disprove a transaction so that the client can get their funds back. When this happens, the vendor hasn't got any option other than gaining their money back. For getting these funds back, the merchant will be charged a transaction fee. Furthermore, if the rate of chargebacks is high, then an additional penalty can be levied on the vendor. Most online sellers have developed better security mechanisms that will help them in detecting fraudulent transactions. In their attempt to reduce chargebacks, the vendors need the buyers to provide them with certain personal information that is considered to be vital for the completion of a transaction. However, this can lead to loss of privacy and a breach of confidentiality as well. The Litecoin network has helped in reversing this situation. Litecoin transactions cannot be reversed intrinsically. Only after a transaction has been validated can it be included in the blockchain, and once this is done, it cannot be reversed. A Litecoin can be tracked by the code that the individual coin possesses. This helps in confirming the authenticity of the currency so that the people who are involved in the transaction won't hesitate to accept the coin as a means of payment. A Litecoin payment once made cannot be replaced without the permission of the vendor. Vendors can now provide and offer their products and services to a wider range of audience without requiring them to divulge any personal information. Litecoins help in improving security and safety of any transaction.

Elimination of middlemen

Middlemen can be quite troublesome when it comes to financial transactions. For instance, there was a time when PayPal had a policy that required an individual to register themselves as a non-profit organization for receiving funds as donations. So, if a user wants to start a crowd-funding program for collecting donations for a charitable cause, they will need to go through the cumbersome process of obtaining the necessary registrations and approvals. By making use of CryptoCurrency, you can skip all these steps. The only two parties involved in a transaction are the buyer and the seller or the sender and the receiver. There is no one else involved. This helps in reducing the costs of transactions as well.

Accepted globally

There are no transactional fees or interests that are levied on cryptocurrencies. This makes cryptocurrencies suitable for international use without any unnecessary hassles. In turn, this will help an individual in saving time and money for conducting transactions online. A user of Litecoins won't have to wait for hours together for conducting an international transfer of funds.

An electronic cash system that isn't owned by a third party. For instance, take a look at PayPal. The company has the inherent power to freeze or suspend a user's account if it feels that the concerned account was misused or used unlawfully. The company can do so without consulting the user. When using CryptoCurrency, you will have a private key that will have a corresponding public key, and this will make up the address of your CryptoCurrency. This cannot be taken away from the user unless the user loses it. CryptoCurrency has a long road ahead of itself before it is capable of replacing traditional forms of currency and credit cards before being accepted as the global commerce tool. By using Litecoins, you can send and receive money anywhere in the world, at any time. You needn't worry about the territorial borders, reschedule according to the bank holidays, or any other limitations that you might have faced when it comes to transferring money. You are in absolute control of your money when it comes to cryptocurrencies since there isn't a particular central authority responsible for the functioning of the network. There are no artificial barriers that might restrict you from trading or make payments to other vendors based in a different part of the world.

Control and security

Litecoins help in letting the users stay in control of the various transactions they enter. Merchants can longer charge an additional fee on a transaction without attracting some attention towards themselves. They will need the prior permission of the client or the customer before any additional charges can be levied on it. When a payment is made using Litecoins, neither of the parties to the transaction will need to divulge any personal information. This helps in protecting personal and sensitive information from the grasp of hackers. Litecoins also help in protecting an individual from any potential identity theft. This CryptoCurrency can be backed up and encrypted. So, the user can make sure that the money is safe. The Litecoin network consists of a large network of computers spread all across the world that are making use of blockchain technology. No centralized authority is responsible for controlling this blockchain network. Decentralization makes sure that control lies within the hands of the users, instead of being concentrated in the hands of a single authority.

Transparency

The blockchain technology that this CryptoCurrency functions on helps in maintaining transparency. All the transactions that have been finalized are available for public viewing. However, certain personal information is well hidden. The public address will be visible, and the personal information is omitted. Any transaction is capable of being verified on the blockchain network. The protocol of the blockchain network cannot be tampered with, and any alterations made to a deal will not go unnoticed. Litecoins are secured cryptographically, and the blockchain technology helps in ensuring transparency of transactions.

Low fees

No fee is levied on payments made with Litecoins, at least not at present and even if there is any, the fee is quite minimal. With routine transactions, a user is bound to incur some transaction charges for the processing of the transaction. The higher the fees paid, the quicker the said transaction will be processed. This doesn't hold true in the case of Litecoins.

Inflationary hedge

There are a finite number of Litecoins that can be created and this limit has been set at 84 million coins. This is said to be a good option in the long run for storing value for providing a hedge against the risk of inflation. This is beneficial for those who reside in countries with extremely volatile rates of inflation. If you must transfer a significant chunk of your income to the Litecoin account, you can isolate yourself from the increasing rates of inflation that plague your local fiat currency. If a vendor isn't accepting Bitcoins as a form of payment, then you can just convert them back into the regular fiat currency for the sake of transacting.

Chapter 3

Risks Involved

Pros and cons coexist in nature. Learning about contradictions will always help you to understand. Litecoins sound pretty good, but like any other type of investment, they have a few inherent risks as well. If you are interested in investing in Litecoins, then it is essential that you are aware of the benefits as well as the risks they possess.

Hacking

Litecoins are electronic currencies that exist on the web. Nowadays, it is easy to hack anything and everything on the Internet. Hacking is a potential risk if you are attacked by cyber-security breaches. Black Hats ideally target crypto currencies due to their vulnerability. Security for holding an underlying currency is comparatively low. If a third party is in charge of your virtual currencies and something goes wrong, you're at a loss. The company or the third party will not offer you help as much as a bank or a card provider will. The protection for a Litecoin or in that case, any virtual currency is less. Investment terms for a virtual currency are different compared to banks or card providers. If you are willing to buy Litecoins, as a customer, you will be charged at higher stakes compared to regular cash.

Threat of being hacked

With a little bit of effort, anything can be hacked, and Litecoin certainly isn't an exception. For instance, hackers managed to steal about $1.2 million in Bitcoins from Inputs.io. The hacking software made use of by the hackers allowed them to find out about the ownership status of the Bitcoins and enabled them to steal all the money. What makes this threat worse is that Litecoin is a lot like cash, in the sense that it can be gone without a trace and it cannot be replaced easily. It is also extremely difficult to recoup any losses if the Litecoin are stolen. This creates the need for an added layer of protection while making use of Litecoin.

However, don't let this discourage you from investing in Litecoin. There are a few things that you will have to do to protect your Litecoins. You should make use of an online wallet, transfer the Litecoins you have earned to an offline wallet or device, and get a cloud storage device that can store the information related to your account in an encrypted format. If you aren't comfortable with any of this, you can always trade in your Litecoin.

It is similar to a commodity

Trading cryptocurrencies is similar to trading commodities. Unlike different investment options like shares or even fixed income securities, cryptocurrencies don't generate any income or dividend. The only manner in which a user can earn money from cryptocurrencies is when there is an increase in its price. So, investing in cryptocurrencies won't suit the requirements of a passive investor.

Lack of regulation

Cryptocurrencies like Litecoin are decentralized. This means that no centralized authority can control or regulate the Litecoin network. In the case of any problem or an issue, the user cannot turn towards a particular authority for grievance redressal.

Likelihood of frauds

Fraud rate and scam rate in crypto currency are high. If you were to invest in a company by following rumors, there is a greater chance that the opportunity is fake. If you decide to buy, please know who you're dealing with. Gather the information of the owner such as his address, his mobile number or his country of residence. Not all virtual currencies are linked to their owner's information. If something goes wrong, you will not be able to contact the owner. The financial crime enforcement network gets you to register and check the information of a Litecoin holder. In few states, the state financial regulators make sure that the exchange is valid.

Privacy

Understanding and analyzing the market is always an asset. Know what an exchange rate is, how is it calculated and its significance. What will you do if an exchange rate is varied at the time of a transaction? If you skip concentrating on fundamentals, then you are increasing your losses. Litecoins are transferred through Litecoin ATM's. The ATM's are connected to the web. Unlike a cash withdrawal ATM, you cannot use Litecoin ATM's to check your balances. The machines charges higher transaction fees - as high as 7%. Virtual currencies are operated by blockchain, a computer network. Research is being carried out on Litecoins, and they are not yet certified. You never know if there's a chance for a completed transaction to be undone. Privacy is a major element. When using Litecoins, the chances of another person knowing your details and your balance coins is high. If your PC's IP address is traced, your entire data can be hacked easily.

Transactions cannot be reversed

As mentioned earlier, vendors don't have to go through the rigorous process of having to validate the integrity of their customers anymore. That responsibility falls on the customer to validate the vendor they are transacting with to ensure that the goods and services that they have paid for with Litecoins are reliable. There are a couple of methods that a customer will have to go through that seem quite complicated. For instance, customers might have to make use of an escrow service provided by a third party to oblige a vendor with the deposit of a performance bond before the Litecoin payment has been made. There can be instances where both the parties involved in the trade might have to take part in an obligatory arbitration of any dispute that crops up. The added effort that is required for the transfer of Litecoins can be problematic.

Volatility of prices

If someone asks you the worth of the Litecoins that you hold currently, will you be able to answer readily? The primary value of a currency depends on the demand of the user and their capability of making use of that currency for transacting trades. Fiat currency depends on the underlying asset that lends value to them. When it comes to CryptoCurrency, their value depends on their demand in the market. Litecoins or any other CryptoCurrency will be considered to be of value as long as the traders and consumers believe so. These currencies are quite volatile. There is a cap on the creation of Litecoins and when this is coupled with the lack of any regulatory body can assist in the manipulation of the prices of Litecoins by the players in the market. The prices of this CryptoCurrency are influenced by the forces of demand and supply. The same forces can also be misused for manipulating these prices. There have been various important speculations made across different online forums on the reason for the manipulation of the prices of Litecoin.

Anti-inflationary

The anti-inflationary nature of these Litecoins can be quite problematic. Only a fixed number of Litecoins can be created, and this criticism is related to this provision. Since there is a limit set, people might want to accumulate this currency instead of spending it. This might decrease the number of Litecoins in circulation.

However, these drawbacks can be overcome easily if you are a prudent investor. Read on to acquire more knowledge about Litecoin and the manner in which you can acquire them.

Chapter 4

Getting Started

If you are interested in investing in Litecoin, then this chapter will provide you with the necessary information for getting started. Here are a couple of things that you should keep in mind while getting started with this CryptoCurrency.

Getting accustomed to Litecoin

If you are used to Bitcoin, then Litecoin will certainly surprise you. The primary desktop application is a modified version of the Bitcoin-OT client. This can be downloaded from the official website of Litecoin, and it can function as a Litecoin wallet as well. More information about Litecoin wallet has been provided in the coming chapters. By now you must be aware of the differences between Litecoin and Bitcoin. Don't worry even if you don't remember; a quick recap will certainly help.

There are 84 Litecoins whereas the cap on Bitcoins is set at 21 million. The initial mining reward for Litecoin was 50 Litecoins per block, and it has come down to 25 Litecoins now. The block time for Litecoin is 2.5 minutes whereas it is 10 minutes for Bitcoin.

Litecoin intelligence

Before you get started with Litecoin investment and trading, you will need to gather all the necessary information. The ecosystem of Litecoin isn't as sophisticated as that of the Bitcoin. Several online sites will help you in making a comparison between LTC and BTC. You can also monitor the growth of LTC against the US dollar. You can join an online forum or community dedicated towards Litecoin. This will help in making sure that you are well informed about everything related to Litecoin.

Buying and trading

The next thing will be to figure out the manner in which you can obtain Litecoin. Unless you are a miner, you will need to buy these from exchanges, forums or in person.

Wallets

The first thing that you will need to do will be to get yourself a wallet for your Litecoins. After this, you will require a place for storing your Litecoin. These wallets are like a regular bank account. Depending on the level of security that you are looking for, different wallets are available. Some are like regular spending accounts that are similar to a regular wallet that you carry with you and then there are others that have a high level of security. Different options are available to you. Most of the wallets have their vulnerabilities. Always make sure that you are storing your Litecoins locally on your computer and back up your wallet regularly so that even if the hard drive gets corrupted, you will still be able to access your account. When it comes to online wallets, make sure that you take all the necessary precautions for securing your Litecoin account from hackers.

Bitcoin exchanges

There are about two-dozen Litecoin exchanges to choose from. There are proper exchanges for institutional traders, and then there are wallet services that are available for someone who is just testing the waters. Most of the exchanges, as well as wallets, will store the digital or fiat currency you hold, just like a traditional bank account would. Exchanges and wallets are a really good option if you ever want to engage in trading. You don't need complete anonymity, and you don't have to take any extensive measures or go through any lengthy procedures that will require the disclosure of contact information and proof of identity. This is pretty much the law regarding trading of Litecoins in most countries, and there is no way in which an exchange can get around this system. These rules are quite similar to the rules that apply to any company that would be interacting with the financial system and would require them to follow the KYC (know your customer) and AML (Anti-money laundering) guidelines. Once you have managed to set up your account, you will need to link your bank account and then make the necessary arrangements for moving these funds between them.

One-on-one meeting

If you live in a big city, you like anonymity, and you don't want to get into the hassles of the banking system, then in such a case, you buy Litecoin from a local seller. There are several online websites and platforms that will help you in reaching out to other Litecoin users and set up meetings with them for buying Litecoins. Remember, if you are meeting someone in person, then you will need to have instant access to your Litecoin wallet and a good Internet connection for cinching the deal. There are a couple of security considerations that buyers and sellers should take while engaging in such trade. Meet in a public place, and don't go around carrying huge amounts of cash. If the concept of a one-on-one meeting doesn't appeal to you, then in such a case you can search for MeetUp groups as well.

Litecoin mining

Litecoin uses a proof-of-work algorithm that is entirely different from the one that Bitcoin makes use of. Litecoin uses Scrypt hashing algorithm. This algorithm was designed in such a manner that it will be difficult to execute a large-scale hardware attack because of the large quantities of memory this would require. Litecoin mining is a complicated process, and it goes beyond simply checking the blocks of Litecoin transactions. Most people end up spending more on the hardware and electricity than they could ever earn from mining. Mining is usually done in pools these days. This means a couple of miners will get together and pool their resources for mining Litecoins and then divide the rewards according to a predetermined ratio. This certainly isn't for hobbyists.

More information about this topic is provided in the coming chapters.

Chapter 5

Litecoin Wallet

This is probably the most important tool that you will need for safeguarding and protecting your Litecoins will be your Litecoin wallet. Like any other type of CryptoCurrency, even Litecoins are capable of being stored in a digital wallet. The wallet will help you in keeping track of the value of the Litecoins you hold and also help you in conducting different transactions. Think of your e-wallet as an email system of sorts, instead of sending and receiving emails; you will be able to send and receive Litecoins. You will also be able to keep track of the history of exchanges and monitor all the transactions.

Types of wallets

Different types of wallets are available, the features that they offer, and their compatibility with devices varies as well. It would be prudent to make yourself aware of the different categories of wallets that are available so that you can choose one that would suit your needs. Wallets are categorized as hot or cold. Those wallets that are connected to the Internet or are available online are referred to as hot. On the other hand, all those wallets that are available offline or aren't connected to the Internet are referred to as cold.

Cold wallets are considered to be secure and are better for storing huge amounts of CryptoCurrency in them. If convenience and accessibility are your priority and if you must frequently access your funds, then in such a case you should opt for the online ones. A good strategy for storing your Litecoins would be to make use of cold storage for all your long-term holdings and a hot wallet for your daily usage. So, let us look at the different types of wallets that you can make use of.

Desktop wallets

These wallets are applications that can be installed or downloaded onto your laptop or your PC. These wallets will be accessible only from a single device, the one on which they have been downloaded. Desktop wallet offers the highest level of security; however, it will be vulnerable if your computer gets hacked or is attacked by a virus. In such a case, you might end up losing all your funds. Desktop wallets are available for different types of OS like Windows, MacOS, and Ubuntu.

Mobile wallet:

A wallet that will run from an app downloaded on your smartphone is referred to as a mobile wallet. This offers convenience and ease of access. These are relatively smaller and simple to use when compared to desktop wallets. Different wallets are available for various operating systems like Android, Windows, and iOS.

Online wallet:

It is a web-based wallet, and it is not available in the form of an app that can be downloaded. It is in the form of data that is stored in a real or virtual server, like the Cloud. It can, therefore, be accessed from any computing device from any location. Some hybrid wallets allow encryption of the private data before it is sent to an online server. Some online wallets have provision for the storage of private keys online and are controlled by third parties, thereby making them vulnerable to hacking and theft.

Exchange-hosted wallet:

This is managed by an exchange or a brokerage like Coinbase or Poloniex for instance. This is different from the wallets mentioned above because you aren't in control of the private keys to your CryptoCurrency stored in them. You will have to place your trust fully in the exchange that is managing it. These wallets do offer services like sending and receiving payments. However, it isn't a wallet in the strict sense of the word. When it comes to managing a lot of funds, it will be better if you make use of any other type of wallet. Exchanges offer convenience by getting rid of the responsibility of securing and backing up the private keys, but this convenience comes at a high cost. Exchanges tend to be the prime targets of hackers. This is quite evident from the failure of two major Bitcoin exchanges like Mt.Gox and Bitfinex.

Hardware wallets:

A hardware wallet is the best way to store all your CryptoCurrency. They are small USB enabled devices for storing your private keys. The benefit of this wallet is that it cannot be hacked. They are designed in such a manner that they can run the wallet software along and nothing else. This makes them immune to malware that the other wallets can fall prey to. However, the only drawback tends to be their cost. These wallets are a little costly, but they are worth the investment.

Paper wallets:

Another cold storage wallet option that you have is to print or even write down the private key on a piece of paper and then lock this up in a safe or a deposit box. You can print the QR code of your public and private key. This will help you in sending and receiving digital currency by using a paper wallet. This method eliminates the need to store digital data about your Litecoins. Online tools can provide key pairs directly on your system, and this can make your keys vulnerable if the site gets hacked. You can also generate keys by making use of the command line, provided you have the required cryptographic packages that have been installed in the preferred language. If you lose your private key, then there is no way in which you can retrieve it once again. If it is gone, then it is gone for good. So, create multiple copies of the QR code and stash them in different secure spots.

Litecoin wallets

Block.io:

This provides a multi-signature wallet to all the Litecoin users. This means that for a transaction to be authorized, two or more signatures will be required. One will be the signature of the user, and the other will be the signature of the company. This also implies that the private keys of every wallet will be stored by the team operating at Block.io and this might be a turn-off for a lot of people. However, it offers more convenience since it supports HD wallet. Apart from Litecoin, it can be used for Bitcoin and Dogecoin as well.

Exodus:

This wallet supports different cryptocurrencies like Litecoin, Bitcoin, Dash, Ether, Dogecoin, and Golem as well. It offers full control to the user over their private keys. It is an open source wallet.

LoafWallet:

If you have a device that can support iOS, then this will be a good option for you. It has all the features that a Litecoin investor will want. A good mobile wallet will cater to the needs of novice and experienced users, and LoafWallet does this. This is a lightweight client, and you don't have to spend hours syncing it with the Blockchain. It makes use of AES hardware encryption and app sandboxing for preventing anyone from inserting their address into a given transaction. What's more? It can be installed onto your Apple Watch as well. If you are looking for functionality, then this is a pretty good option.

Electrum-LTC:

This is a popular wallet amongst Bitcoin users. Now, they have tweaked the codebase for supporting Litecoin too. It makes use of a set passphrase for protecting a wallet and for restoring a wallet from a backup. It can be downloaded for devices supported by Linux, Windows, and OSX from the official online site. This is a lightweight wallet, and therefore you needn't wait for hours to sync it with the blockchain. The main advantage of this wallet is its backup feature. Even if the user does lose their Electrum-LTC wallet, it can be retrieved in the app by using the passphrase. There is an option of generating offline wallet for cold storage. Users can also export the address of their private key to another Litecoin wallet.

When you are selecting a wallet for securing your CryptoCurrency, make sure that you are prudent.

Chapter 6

Buying Litecoin

In this chapter, you will learn about the different ways in which you can buy Litecoins by making use of various payment options. Before you get started with buying Litecoins, you should make sure that you have got a good wallet in which you can store your Litecoins.

Buying with credit or debit card

Coinbase: This is perhaps the easiest manner in which you will be able to buy Litecoins with your credit card. The purchase fee that is charged is up to 3.99% of a given purchase. This platform is available in US, UK, Europe, Singapore, and Australia. This same platform can also be made use of for buying Litecoins with a bank account or a bank transfer. This option is available in all the countries mentioned above and Canada as well. Americans can make use of ACH transfer (it'll take about 5 to 7 days), and Europeans can make use of SEPA transfer and the waiting period can range from a day to three days. The fees per transaction are about 1.49%.

Bitpanda: This is based in Austria, and it is a crypto-brokerage service. Residents of most of the European countries can buy Litecoins by accessing this platform. SEPA can be made use of for transfer from any of the European countries. NETELLER, GiroPay, or SOFORT can be made use of as well for a bank transfer.

Buying Litecoin with cash

There is no good way in which you can buy Litecoins with cash. The most popular manner for acquiring Bitcoins instead of cash would be via LocalBitcoins. However, this platform doesn't support Litecoin as of now. The other Bitcoin exchanges that are quite popular are BitQuick and Wall of Coins, and neither of these is Litecoin compatible. This means that you will need to first purchase Bitcoins with cash and then exchange these for Litecoin by making use of the methods mentioned above. The same will apply to Bitcoin ATMs as well. Most of them don't support Litecoin. So, if you are interested in buying Litecoin at a Bitcoin ATM, you will need to purchase Bitcoin and then convert them into Litecoin.

Buying Litecoin with PayPal

Just like buying Litecoin with cash, there is no direct way in which you can buy Litecoin with PayPal. You will have to acquire Bitcoin by making use of PayPal, and once you have acquired Bitcoins, you will need to convert them into Litecoin. The process of acquiring Bitcoin with PayPal is quite extensive.

Buying Litecoin with Bitcoin

If you are already in possession of Bitcoins, then it is very easy to convert these into Litecoins. You will need to find an exchange that deals in LTC/BTC transactions. Most of the exchanges deal in such transactions because they are quite popular.

Changelly:

This is perhaps the fastest method that is available for the conversion of Bitcoin to Litecoin. You will simply have to enter the number of Litecoin you will want to buy and provide the Litecoin address. Then this platform does the calculations and will inform you the number of Bitcoins that will be necessary for the exchange and the address to which the Bitcoins should be sent. Once you do this, the LTC will be automatically sent to your wallet after a little while.

Buying Litecoin with Skrill

BiPanda also accepts Skrill payments for acquiring Litecoins. The fee will vary and will be included in your buying price.

Buying Litecoin with Ethereum

2017 has been quite a lucky year for Ethereum, and this CryptoCurrency has witnessed a massive surge in its prices. Ethereum holders can trade in their ether for buying Litecoin. Litecoin has a very good rate of liquidity, and it is quite popular among traders, especially in China. In this section, let us take a look at some of the popular exchanges that you can make use of for converting your Ethereum into Litecoin.

Changelly:

This is perhaps the most unique exchange there is, and it is also a fast way in which you can convert Ethereum into Litecoin. When you are making use of Changelly, you needn't have to store your money with the exchange (third-party), and this reduces your exposure to the risk of theft. You will simply have to specify the number of Litecoin you want to buy, specify the address to which the Litecoin needs to be sent. Changelly will do the calculations and will inform you of the number of Ethereum that will be required for this purchase. They will provide an address to which Ether will need to be sent, and within a while, you will receive a deposit of Litecoin to your wallet. Any other form of altcoin can also be converted to Litecoin by making use of Changelly, and the same procedure is applicable.

Poloniex:

This is the largest exchange of altcoin in the world. There is one major drawback of making use of Poloniex for converting your Ethereum to Litecoin. Poloniex does not directly assist in the conversion of Ethereum to Litecoin. You will first have to convert your Ethereum to Bitcoin and then convert this Bitcoin to Litecoin. This method does work, but it isn't cost effective. There are multiple trades that are involved, and this means that the cost of transaction fees involved will be on the higher side as well.

ShapeShift:

This is quite similar to Changelly. In fact, this was the first company that had come up with the concept of exchange for holding onto your funds.

The most frequently asked question about the conversion of Ethereum to Litecoin is "why are there only a few options available?" The basic issue present in all of the crypto markets across the globe is liquidity. As the space increases, the liquidity will also improve. However, as of now, Bitcoin is the only CryptoCurrency that enjoys a high rate of liquidity. The other cryptocurrencies will soon follow suit. This is the main reason why most of the options regarding the purchase of Litecoin require Bitcoin and then its conversion or exchange.

Buying Litecoin online

Most of the options that have been mentioned above will allow you to buy Litecoins online. You will have to buy them online if you want to acquire them by making use of your credit card, debit card, bank transfer, or even Skrill. The only option where an online transfer isn't possible is when you are trying to buy them with cash.

Frequently Asked Questions

In this section, let us take into consideration some frequently asked questions about Litecoins. Anyone who is just getting started with Litecoins will have one or several of the questions that have been discussed in this section.

What are the risks involved while buying Litecoins?

The one risk that you need to be aware of while you are buying Litecoin is that its price can plummet down to zero. This means that you will lose your money. Also, the other risk involved would be leaving your money on an exchange or a similar platform.

Why does it take long to buy Litecoin?

The legacy banking system is the main reason why it takes a while for buying Litecoin. This system is quite slow. If you are buying Litecoin with the help of any other CryptoCurrency, then this process is quicker. A bank transfer in the US, for instance, takes about five days for completion. So, if you want to purchase any Litecoin within the US via a bank transfer, then this transaction will take five days for completion.

Can Litecoin be sold?

Most of the exchanges that have been mentioned above allow the user to sell Litecoins as well. If you can buy them, then you most certainly can sell them as well. There will be a certain fee that might be levied.

Can a buyer buy partial Litecoins?

Yes, if you want to, you can buy partial Litecoin as well. Just like Bitcoin, even Litecoin can be divisible to multiple decimal places. This means that you are allowed to buy 0.1 Litecoin, 0.01 Litecoin, and so on.

Can anyone purchase Litecoins or are there any restrictions?

No, there are no restrictions placed on this and anyone can buy Litecoins. Provided the potential buyer has managed to find an exchange for the same that supports Litecoin in the country he resides in. Most of the CryptoCurrency wallets don't need an ID for signing up. So, it is quite easy to create your wallet and get started with acquiring

Litecoins as long as you have got the means to do so.

Should I mine or buy Litecoins?

If you have got access to cheap electricity, then it will be worth your while to mine Litecoins. If you have access to solar power or if you want to mine because you are a hobbyist, then this might be appealing to you. If not, it is better that you buy Litecoin. Mining is a dynamic process, and its level of difficulty keeps on increasing. The worth of a Litecoin and the sum of all the expenses you will need to incur will affect your profitability. More information about mining has been provided in the next chapter.

What is the best payment method?

If speed is your primary criterion, then transfer via credit card will be the fastest method of acquiring Litecoins. If you are transacting in large amounts, then you should consider bank transfer. For the sake of privacy, the best method to use will be to purchase Bitcoin and then convert or trade these for Litecoins on different exchanges.

What can I do with Litecoins?

As soon as you acquire Litecoins, make sure that you are transferring these to a secure wallet. You shouldn't leave your Litecoins just sitting on an exchange for long. There have been different instances where Bitcoin networks were hacked. Once you lose your CryptoCurrency, there is no way in which you can recover them again. Losing your precious Litecoin due to security breaches or hacking can be quite a blow.

Chapter 7

Litecoin Mining

Just like Bitcoin, Litecoin is an online network that can be made use of for online transactions. Litecoin is a peer-to-peer network that is decentralized. The payment system comprises of its unit, referred to as Litecoin and this is different from fiat currency. Just like Bitcoin, even Litecoin can be mined. In this chapter, you will learn more about Litecoin mining.

What is Litecoin mining?

Litecoin works on a decentralized network. No central authority will be responsible for securing and controlling the supply of money. This work is spread across a network of "miners." All the new transactions that appear on the Litecoin network are organized into large bundles that are referred to as "blocks." These blocks, when put together, will comprise a reliable system of all the transactions that were ever made and is collectively called the "blockchain." These blocks are difficult to produce, and this ensures that there is only one blockchain on the Litecoin network. So, instead of being able to produce blocks at will, miners will need to generate a cryptographic hash for a block that will meet a few conditions, and the only way to do this will be by computing different blocks and find that one code that will work. This process is known as hashing. Whenever a miner creates a block, the reward given for doing this is 25 Litecoins. Every couple of days, the difficulty criteria for the hash is adjusted depending upon the frequency of the appearance of the blocks. There is a direct relationship between the competition and the work that is necessary for finding a block. This means that the greater the level of competition amongst the miners, the more effort will is necessary for determining a block.

Mining Litecoins, a sustainable profit or a marginal loss

Uncertainty in market conditions makes way for losses. However, when mining Litecoins, these losses can be turned into profits. Previous generations followed the trend of making profits by mining CPUs and GPU's. In today's world, the introduction of ASIC's – a specialized mining technique has changed the way of dealing with hardware. Regarded as an effective, efficient and swift method of mining, ASIC is harder to use for general-purpose hardware.

A comparison of a CPU, a GPU, and an ASIC reveals that each method yields profits. But in the case of a CPU and a GPU, the marginal profits obtained when offered with free rewards such as electricity are considerably less. You cannot invest your hard effort into something that yields less profit. ASIC's hardware is not completely reliable either.

Don't worry. By mastering the basics and considering various elements, you can get far better results. Some of the most important factors are stated here.

- Electricity and Power. Limit your usage so that you can save some credit. One should not pay more than he/she earns. That's a loss!
- Competition. Once people know that mining can fetch profits, many of them will join the mining network. With high traffic and demand, don't lose control of your principles. Try to assume the worst-case scenario and work for survival.
- Buying and Selling. ASIC is one effective and efficient mining technique that can buy you Litecoins. The sole purpose of buying is to sell when the demand increases. But ASIC cannot help in selling at the best prices. Resale value of an ASIC is comparatively less.
- Delays. Make sure that you receive the pre-ordered mine on time. Most of the miners' face

difficulty with delivery dates. What use is it if your hardware is not delivered to you when you need it?

Never rely on a single source of information. This isn't the Stone Age. Surf the web and gather all the information you can. I suggest you visit www.Litecoinpool.org and also https://www.coindesk.com/information/how-to-mine-Litecoin/ as an initiative.

Is it a must that you should be a miner in-order to invest in hardware? No. You can kick-off with Litecoins by purchasing them at an exchange.

Mining Pools

A pool is a source of gathered information. As stated above, the website www.Litecoinpool.org is a mining pool where you can find information on Litecoin mining. As an individual miner, it takes you several months to find a block. Though you own powerful hardware, without mining pools you are lost. When the information is shared, it travels fast enough enabling you to find blocks at ease. A pool user gives in his work with valid proofs. In return, he earns shares/Litecoins as his rewards. The rewards may increase or decrease depending on the value of information that the user has provided in solving a block.

The rewards are categorized into two different systems namely Proportional Systems and Pay-Per-Share Systems.

- Proportional Systems. These are group/round-based systems. One user in the pool does the work in finding a block. Needed information on the block is provided by the remaining users of the group. Once the user finds the block, the reward is distributed among the group depending on the number of shares each user has offered. In this system, malpractices are frequent. Pool Hopping is a major disadvantage in using the Proportional system. To eradicate this, more efficient versions like PPS are followed.

- Pay-Per-Share. In this system, work of the user in finding a block is rewarded. The amount of work done by a user in a pool to find a given number of blocks within a deadline is considered. Litecoins are paid as rewards for each valid share submitted by the user. Pay-Per-Share system follows Probabilities law of Mathematics. Regular payoffs and fewer variations in the pool make this system user-friendly. The risk of bad luck needs to be taken up by the pool operator. PPS at times can be a risk in financial terms.

Deciding the right pool is a vital point. Factors such as features, reliability, reputation, rating and user support must be carefully considered when joining a pool.

Which software suits the best for mining?

Let's begin with CPU mining. You know that this technique doesn't fetch high profits. Yet you want to give it a shot because it doesn't yield losses either. The first step will be to download pooler's CPU miner, Pooler's software from https://github.com/pooler/cpuminer. You can find the next steps, i.e. connecting to a pool, on the website. For any assistance, please find the required information on the help page.

If you opt for GPU mining, it is a bit tougher than CPU mining. As the setup is harder and it is less effective, it is not really such a good idea. If you're interested, https://minergate.com/altminers/claymore-gpu will provide you all the required information.

An ASIC has preinstalled software on an integrated controller. The setup is straightforward and doesn't have any configuration either. As a part time miner, it is a very bad idea to buy a costly ASIC processor. Instead, you can use your in-home desktop or laptop to start mining Bitcoins and Litecoins.

Let us take a look at the manner in which you can get started with mining crypto currencies such as

Litecoins and Bitcoins without expensive equipment.

SHA-256 or Scrypt have widely used algorithms in CryptoCurrency mining. SHA-256 is an efficient algorithm yet most of the miners prefer Scrypt. Scrypt, a modern- day algorithm, can provide proof-of-work quite efficiently. Apart from its efficiency, Scrypt has more memory storage and can work on any platform. A regular PC with minimum graphics is best suited for Scrypt, while SHA-256 needs dedicated ASIC's.

This might come as a surprise to some of you and a shock to others. But yes, you can use your PCs to mine digital currencies. The efficiency of this software may not be that effective when compared to that of a processor. But by saving your money and time in investing in a Processor, it is recommended that you start mining on your PC.

Wallets as Storages

Currency is stored in wallets. And the same applies to Litecoins as well. As already mentioned in the Storing Bitcoins Section, all that you need is to ready your wallets for storing your Litecoins. Many options/software is available for storing your currency. It is recommended that a beginner should make use of LiteVault or CoinsBank for a wallet. A default wallet application can be found on the homepages readily available for download. Please do your research by referring to different forums or blogs. Many active communities are available on the web that will help you in getting a kick-start. Most of the wallets are incorporated from Bitcoins clients. So, a lengthy procedure must be followed to make your downloads. Please Be Patient. Refer to the previous chapters if you need more information about different wallets.

Speed

If you do not own a mining hardware such as a processor, you still have two other ways of mining these crypto-currencies. One procedure can be performed with your Central-Processing-Unit (CPU) while the other uses your Graphics-Processing-Unit (GPU). A GPU depends on your graphic card. So, it's entirely up to you to decide which procedure should be followed.

Taking Cryptographic calculations into account, the GPU offers an outstanding performance. If you are about to start mining for Litecoins for the first time, do it on your desktop. NVidia and Radeon offer better performance depending on your PC's configuration. The mining rate depends on the configuration of the system. If you start mining on an Intel PC, you will mine at a slower rate.

An Intel Motherboard doesn't offer much to the miners. For this sole purpose, external graphics are available on the market. To support the speed at a regular rate, most miners build a dedicated machine, maybe a virtual one using motherboards and riser cables. If you aren't interested in building your mining rig, you can perhaps buy one!

The temperature in the room rises when you start mining. The system should serve intensively. In this process, the life of your equipment is reduced. Make sure to make regular checks and do not allow the temperatures to rise too high. Uphold your warranties just in case and try to preserve the equipment by regulating the temperature of the place in which it is used. Make sure that the room in which you have placed the mining equipment is quite cold. This is the main reason why mining is said to take up a lot of electricity.

Individual effort or Group Work?

Mining can be an individual's play or a group work, i.e. a pool, where information is exchanged at higher rates. Mining Pools are regarded as lotteries. Profits and losses coexist. If you're solo, it means you get to keep the full credit. But the chances of finding a block solo is low - in fact, 0.1%. While in a pool, you will surely locate the block, but the rewards are split among the group members for their contributions. You can earn more only if you can share more information. That's how it works in a team.

As a beginner, configuring the hardware and the software and finding information on a block will be the hardest part. But, a beginner can easily join a pool. Rewards will not be high as soon as you join. As you grow in a group, the chances of getting higher reward increases. Steady incomes will generate as long as you find blocks.

Deciding on which currency to be mined is also a critical point. Pools and multi- pools will ensure the profitability and help you decide on mining the profitable opportunities.

Installation of Central-Processing-Unit Miner

https://github.com/pooler/cpuminer provides you with the CPU-miner application. CPU-miner is the best and easiest way to start mining. CPU-Miner requires the usage of the command line on your desktop. The application on the website supports both 32 bit and 64-bit platforms, and it is compatible with Windows, Mac and also Linux. Windows is widely used around the world, and I assume that even you are using Windows. For any other operating systems, please download and extract the ZIP file. Creating a shortcut on your desktop will enable you to access the software at ease.

Coding your script

As discussed earlier, a command line is needed to start mining software. Let me elaborate the procedure for writing a code that starts your software. The parameters required for mining a pool are mentioned below. In Windows, a batch file is used to initiate the mining application. A batch file has a one-line script where the user can create/modify the existing script.

Requirements to launch the miner.

1. The installation directory and the path where the miner application is installed. Example: a.

Installation directory: C:\cpu-miner-pooler
b. Path: minerd.exe.
2. The Link or the web address of your mining pool server. Example: stratum+tcp://pool.d2.cc.
3. Mining server's Port number. It usually has digits in sequential order such as 548407.
4. Username with which you are registered on the mining pool. Example: skj2109.
5. Your Worker's Name or Working Number. Example: 26 or Mitch.
6. Your Worker Password. Example: Icannotrevealmine.

Now, it's time to enter the scripting algorithm, Scrypt. Use a text editor or a note pad for this purpose. However, applications like MS Word cannot be used to enter the scripting algorithm. Now Enter the formula as follows:

Formula:

Start "path" minerd.exe - -URL URL:PORT –a Scrypt - - userpass USERNAME.WORKER:PASSWORD

Using the above examples, the formula looks like this.

Start "C:\cpu-miner-pooler" minerd.exe --url stratum+tcp://pool.d2.cc:548407 -a scrypt --userpass skj2109.26:icannotrevealmine

Now, save the document with a .batch extension. Example – Mining.bat. After saving the batch file, run it by double clicking on the mining.bat. This activates the mining operation. The mining pool has a web interface, and in few minutes your mining worker's account will turn to the active state.

Once your account is activated, you can start looking for information and explore blocks. That looks simple. Let us now take a detailed look at the complex method of GPU mining.

Graphical-Processing-Unit Mining.

Mining with GPU or USB devices is a bit complex. The CG-Miner application can serve this purpose at its best. https://minergate.com/altminers/claymore-gpu helps you to download the application. However, a CG-Miner doesn't have a developed site for Mac versions. If you are a Mac user, please find in the binaries from https://github.com/dmaxl/cgminer. CG-Miner has many versions, and version 3.72 doesn't support Scrypt Mining. In version 3.82, the support for GPU's was entirely removed. This gives you the opportunity to download the version that suits you instead of the latest release.

Following through with the assumption that you are using a Windows OS. The command line arguments are the same for all the version of Operating systems available. In Mac and Linux, don't forget to download and extract the ZIP file. In GPU mining, let us mine using a Scrypt currency again.

Firstly, extract the software into a file on the desktop for ease of access. Example: C:\desktop\Mining\cgminer\. Before moving on to the next step, make sure that all the graphic drivers are up to date. Now, open the start menu and search for a run option. A Run pop-up opens. Type cmd, command prompt and press Enter. You can also follow the short cut by pressing 'Windows + R' buttons at the same time. A command prompt window pops open. Now, change the directory to the location of the downloaded cgminer ZIP file.

Type 'cgminer.exe – n' and press enter. This command will list out all the devices recognized by your PC. If the graphic card is detected in the list of devices, you can happily continue to the further step. If the graphic card is not detected, then please open the control panel and search for the graphic card. Uninstall and reinstall the drivers and try again. If the problem persists, please refer to forums on the web to solve this issue.

www.playtool.com/pages/troubleshooting/intro.html will help you in fixing graphic card troubles.

Repeat the same procedure as followed in CPU mining for mining the pool.

Requirements to launch the miner are mentioned as follows:

1. The installation directory and the path where the miner application is installed. Example: a. Installation directory: C:\cg-miner-pooler b. Path: minerd.exe.
2. The Link or the web address of your mining pool server. Example: stratum+tcp://pool.d2.cc.
3. Mining server's Port number. It usually has digits in sequential order such as 548407.
4. Username with which you are registered on the mining pool. Example: skj2109.
5. Your Worker's Name or Working Number. Example: 26 or Mitch.
6. Your Worker Password. Example: Icannotrevealmine.

Now, it's time to enter the scripting algorithm, Scrypt. Use a text editor or a note pad for this purpose. However, applications like MS Word cannot be used to enter the scripting algorithm. Now Enter the formula as follows:

Formula you can use

start "path" minerd.exe - -URL URL:PORT –a scrypt - - userpass USERNAME.WORKER:PASSWORD

Using the above examples, the formula looks like this.

start "C:\cg-miner-pooler" minerd.exe --URL stratum+tcp://pool.d2.cc:548407 -a scrypt --userpass skj2109.26:icannotrevealmine

Looking out for Miner

Now that the software is setup and the script is coded, various statistics and lines will show up scrolling along your command prompt. A CG-miner produces more information than a CPU-miner. A CG miner can display the information about currency, mining pool as well as the mining hardware. A CPU miner can produce only the information of the references to the blocks found and solved. A CPU miner also shows the speed of the solution i.e. hashing speed.

Improve the efficiency

A processor can run both Central processing unit mining and Graphical processing unit mining at the same time. Here's the good news folks, a PC with good graphic performance also has the same capacity. Remember the code for miners? Edit this code by adding '—threads n' argument to the command prompt of minerd.exe. 'n' stands for the number of CPU cores the user wants to accommodate to the mining strategy.

Do leave one or two cores free to control Graphical-processing units (GPU's). Configuring miner without leaving out cores will put more pressure on the central processing unit (CPU). The CPU has to send data to the GPU for processing at the same time it mines for itself. For example, you own an octa-core processor. An octa core processor has 8 cores. If you try to edit 4 threads, then 4 cores will continue CPU mining, and the remaining 4 will take care of GPU mining.

CPU and GPU mining when activated at the same time reveal the best and the most effective procedure. As you have already learned, GPU mining is way better than CPU mining but has a complicated installation procedure. Hash rates are efficient outputs of mining. When CPU hash rates are compared with GPU's, the difference will be at least five times.

Mining isn't a simple process, and it will take you a while to get the hang of it. Before you can get started with it, you need to make sure that you have all the essential equipment for doing so. If you want to join a mining pool, make sure that the rules regarding profit sharing are discussed and established well in advance. Mining can be a stressful and an incredibly lengthy process. So, you will need to be patient. Your luck matters too!

Chapter 8

Tips for Investing

Irrespective of whether you are investing in the stock market, real estate, or in cryptocurrencies, you will need to set some safety rules for yourself. Losing the Litecoins you hold can be a costly mistake. There are certain mistakes that investors tend to make when dealing in cryptocurrencies. There are two things that every investor needs to concentrate on to make a good trade and these are 100% focus and setting of certain ground rules. Think of these ground rules as tips for investing.

Have a reason

You will need a reason before you enter a trade. Start a business only when you are aware of the reason and have a clear strategy in your mind. This is a zero-sum game (if one individual benefits, then someone else will be cutting their losses). Understand that not every trader can earn a profit.

The market for cryptocurrencies is driven by all those who are willing to buy and sell. The sellers and the buyers constitute the market. Even if you want to trade on a daily basis, the one thing that you should understand is that, at times, not earning a profit is better than suffering a loss. So, make sure that you have a good reason before you start trading. At times, the only way in which you can hold onto your profits is by not doing anything.

Stop-loss

For every trade you make or enter into, you will need a clear target for the level of profit that you can take and a stop-loss for cutting your losses. A stop-loss setting is the level of loss after which you should exit the trade. There are a couple of things that you should take into consideration before you set your stop-loss level. Most traders tend to fail when they get attached to a coin or a trade. They might keep going with the false belief that things might just take a turn for the better at any given point of time and that they will be able to get out of a trade unscathed or with minimum loss. Don't let your ego get the better of you and don't let it control your trading decisions. Crypto trades are certainly a lot riskier than the regular trades in a stock market. A coin's worth can rise exponentially and plummet towards zero quite quickly and without warning.

Fear of missing out

The fear of missing out is quite real. It isn't fun to simply be witness to a situation where a particular CryptoCurrency is doing well and is gaining value quite rapidly. Most of the time, investors tend to follow a trend just because they do not want to miss out on an opportunity. At times, it is better just to observe the way the market is functioning.

Risk management

Always be upfront about the amount of risk you can shoulder. There is no point in jumping into a risky trade only to suffer a loss. Know the limit of your exposure towards loss and play within this range.

Homework

Try to learn as much as possible before stepping into the market. Knowledge is infinite and powerful. Don't just learn about trading procedures, but learn about news and events that may have a significant effect on markets. Follow news regularly to make sure that you are well aware of all the changes that are taking place in the world of CryptoCurrency. Learning about a particular CryptoCurrency before getting started will help you in making an informed decision.

General tips

Here are a couple of general tips that will come in handy when you are stepping into the world of CryptoCurrency trading.

The first thing that you should figure out will be the objective or the purpose for which you have taken up trading. Determining the motivating factor will influence all your trading decisions, so you need to get this right. The next step will be the description of the strategy you have opted for. Describe your strategy and the trading process.

Once you have done this, you will need to perform a strategic analysis of the market. This means you will need to carefully analyze the CryptoCurrency and the markets in which you want to trade.

The next step will be a feasibility analysis. The CryptoCurrency options you are going for should be feasible for you. You will need to determine the resources you have on hand and the amount of loss that you can afford to incur. Resources will include time, money and effort that you are willing to invest.

You need to think about the psychological elements of the plan. This means you need to analyze yourself to see whether you are prepared to start investing or not. You will need to keep a positive attitude and shouldn't give up at the first sign of trouble. There are bound to be some losses that you will suffer; it is all about your ability to bounce back into the game.

The operational plan will help you in figuring out what you will need to do to implement your plan.

The last thing that you will need to find out will be the financial plan. You will need to think about the financial resources that you have at your disposal; the amount of money you will need for trading, the money you can afford to risk, and the loss that you can afford to suffer.

These general tips will help in making sure that you are on the right track when it comes to investing in cryptocurrencies. One thing that you always need to remember is that you should stick to your plan and don't get carried away with your emotions.

Other Books from the Author

To check out Jeff's latest books visit his Amazon author site or go here:

http://bit.ly/JeffReedBooks

- ✓ *Blockchain: The Essential Guide to Understanding the Blockchain Revolution*
- ✓ *Fintech: Financial Technology and Modern Finance in the 21st Century*
- ✓ *Investing in Ethereum: The Essential Guide to Profiting from Cryptocurrencies*
- ✓ *Smart Contracts: The Essential Guide to Using Blockchain Smart Contracts for Cryptocurrency Exchange*

www.ingramcontent.com/pod-product-compliance
Lightning Source LLC
Chambersburg PA
CBHW070308230526
45470CB00002B/782